Original title:
Fieldwork in Free Verse

Copyright © 2025 Creative Arts Management OÜ
All rights reserved.

Author: Dorian Ashford
ISBN HARDBACK: 978-1-80566-710-0
ISBN PAPERBACK: 978-1-80566-995-1

Explorations of a Breathless Journey

With my map upside down, I stroll,
Chasing butterflies that outsmart my goals.
Each turn a riddle, each step a prank,
I laugh at blunders, my compass sank.

Muddy socks and a tangled hair,
I trip on roots that sneak like a bear.
The sun's my spotlight, oh how I shine,
As I dance with shadows, feeling divine.

Canvas of the Living Landscape

Nature's palette, vibrant and bold,
A snail's slow race, now that's pure gold.
I paint with laughter, colors of glee,
While the ants host a banquet—a sight to see!

Dandelion wishes float through the air,
I blow them gently—my secret to share.
Grass tickles my feet, a soft serenade,
As I wonder if nature too feels afraid.

The Language of Rustling Leaves

Leaves gossip as they shimmy and sway,
Whispers of secrets they flutter away.
A squirrel debates if to climb or to stay,
While I ponder snacks for a festive buffet.

Branches waltz as if holding a trance,
I join the charade, what a clumsy dance!
Nature's own chatter, a comedic show,
I chuckle at life—the best kind of flow.

Catching Glimpses of Solitude

In solitude's arms, I lay on the grass,
Staring at clouds, letting moments pass.
A thought floats by, then it takes a dive,
Was that a cow? Oh, it's just a hive!

The breeze carries jokes, tickling my brain,
While shadows tease me, playing their game.
With each awkward giggle, I find my joy,
In this quiet escape, I'm a carefree boy.

Sketches in the Dust

In the heat, I draw lines,
A stick figure waving hi.
My pencil's lost in sand,
It asks, 'Where's my eraser?'

A crow has claimed my snack,
With a caw and a flap.
I bargain with the sky,
But it just laughs back.

Unraveled Threads of Green

I trip on a vine,
It seems to giggle loud.
Nature plays a prank,
I'm the jester, how proud!

Frogs croak in a chorus,
They've got rhythm, you see.
They hop like musicians,
With no tickets to flee.

The Language of the Lost

A squirrel gives a lecture,
About nuts and their worth.
I nod like I understand,
He chitters, full of mirth.

A beetle walks in circles,
With plans he can't quite tell.
I offer him a map,
He rolls it up so well!

Footprints in the Silence

I wandered through the quiet,
My shoes left prints like art.
A rabbit jumps beside me,
With a thump that breaks my heart.

In the hush, a whisper,
'Chase me, if you can!'
I stumble and I laugh,
And draw a line in sand.

Between the Rustling Grass

Amidst the blades, a mystery shrieks,
A lost sheep bleats, while the rooster sneaks.
I chase a butterfly, it mocks my haste,
With every flutter, my plans laid to waste.

A grasshopper laughs, jumps high with glee,
While I'm tangled up, like a kite in a tree.
The sun smiles down, a witness to my plight,
Nature's comedy, a never-ending flight.

The Absent Poet's Guide

He left me notes, in a muddle of ink,
About cow-shaped clouds and the way bugs blink.
But when I look, all I see are crows,
Dancing like poets with giant prose.

Where's the wisdom in a wandering breeze?
It swirls my hat, with effortless ease.
I jot down dreams of improbable sights,
Yet here I am, in the middle of flights.

Singularity of the Sky

The sun and moon dance, what a curious sight,
They argue over who brings more light.
Stars spill secrets over the wind's embrace,
While I trip on pebbles in this cosmic race.

A shooting star zips, a comet in tow,
What is this show? Just go with the flow.
With each wink above, a story unfolds,
Between humor and wonder, this sky never grows old.

Lanterns of Forgotten Stories

Down winding paths, lanterns bob and sway,
Illuminating tales from yesterday.
I stumble upon laughter, lost in the night,
As shadows share whispers, a curious sight.

An old tree chuckles, bending with age,
Its roots entwined in a whimsical stage.
I gather the giggles, tuck them away,
For in these fragments, I find my way.

Soliloquy of the Meadow

A cow chews grass, lost in thought,
Dreaming of fields where daisies fought.
The ants parade, a tiny brigade,
While I trip over roots, a grand charade.

The sunshine winks through leaves so green,
Tickling my toes, oh what a scene!
Bumblebees buzz with gossip untold,
While I fumble, a sight to behold!

Mosaic of Wandered Landscapes

A squirrel stashes nuts with great flair,
Creating a stash for a long winter stare.
The brook sings a tune, splashing with glee,
I slip on a rock, it's a comedy spree!

Clouds drift like sheep in the big blue sky,
As I stumble along, trying hard not to fly.
A deer pops out, raises a brow,
I salute it, all awkward, and somehow vow.

A Chronicle of Untold Seasons

The leaves fall like confetti from trees,
I dance through the mess, if you please.
Raccoons peek out, judging my moves,
While I try to impress with my silly grooves.

Winter arrives with a frosty grin,
Hot cocoa in hand, let the fun begin!
Snowballs fly, and so do my socks,
I land in a drift, the crowd mocks!

Gathering Starlight and Dew

The moon laughs brightly, in a silvery dress,
As I trip over roots, I can't help but confess.
Crickets chirp like they're crafting a tune,
While I hum along to the light of the moon.

The morning brings dew, all shiny and bright,
Dancing on grass, what a glorious sight!
I dash for a sip, a risky endeavor,
And land in a puddle—oh, I'm clever!

The Unraveled Narrative of Nature

In muddy boots, we stumble and slip,
Chasing squirrels on an acorn trip.
The trees gossip in the rustling breeze,
While I swear that one just called me a tease.

A butterfly flirts, but it's just a tease,
Leading me on with a flutter and freeze.
I take a step, find myself in a hole,
And all I can see is the sky—oh, the toll!

Mapping the Invisible

With a compass that spins like a child's top,
I chase the shadows, making them hop.
The map's all scribbles, lines crisscrossed,
Like my brain when I think, all logic tossed.

Let's measure the breeze, oh that's a fine goal,
I'll capture a breeze with a jar, oh so bold!
But it slips out like laughter, oh what a tease,
I'm left with just whispers and a tickling sneeze!

Beyond the Ant's Chorus

A parade of ants with a purpose so grand,
Marching in lines that I can't understand.
They throw me a glance, I swear it's a glare,
Do they think I'm a threat or just unaware?

I tried to join their march, what a sight to behold,
But tripped on a twig, oh the shame I uphold.
The queen gave a sigh, rolled her antennae with flair,
While I lay in the grass, pretending not to care.

Capturing the Flicker of Wings

With a net made of hopes and a heart full of glee,
I aim for the butter that flits by the tree.
But my swipes are quite clumsy, a butterfly giggles,
I chase its bright colors; it dances and wiggles.

I trip on a root, land smack on my face,
While it flutters away, unbothered, with grace.
The flowers all chuckle, they know all my tricks,
Nature's got jokes; they're just in the mix!

Echoes of the Unseen

In the woods, a squirrel talks,
Laughing at my startled sneeze.
Leaves whisper secrets of the lost,
I can't tell if it's just the breeze.

Raccoons play hide and seek,
With my lunch, they think it's fair.
They dance around, those furry thieves,
Leaving me with just a glare.

A chipmunk munches on my snack,
Pausing, glances, then dashes away.
I swear he winked, a cheeky rogue,
Who knew lunch could end this way?

I'm the clown in nature's show,
They giggle as I trip and fall.
In this grand comedy of life,
I'm just the punchline after all.

Mapping the Heartbeat of Nature

Today I tracked a wayward bee,
Using breadcrumbs for a map.
It buzzed with laughter, then flew off,
Right into my peanut butter trap.

A deer called out, "I need a guide!"
As I stumbled over roots and vines.
I told her, "No, I'm lost, you see,"
She rolled her eyes, searching for signs.

The owls hoot with their wise old jokes,
While the frogs croak with ribbit and cheer.
Nature's laughter, loud and bright,
Who knew the woods could be so queer?

With each step, I scribble notes,
But the squirrels seem to laugh it off.
Mapping this chaos of joy and mayhem,
I'm just a researcher, or so they scoff.

Beneath the Canopy of Dreams

Underneath the leafy roof,
A mushroom jokes about my hat.
"Too big!" it says with a cheeky smile,
While a spider learns to twirl like that.

A raccoon juggles acorns with flair,
While I'm busy dodging a flighty bat.
I try to take notes, but it's hard to write,
When laughter echoes where I sat.

The sun tickles the branches above,
While grasshoppers lead a dancing team.
They hop and sway, and I can't resist,
Join the rhythm of nature's dream.

In this world where silliness reigns,
I find joy in the simplest things.
Among the flora, fauna, and fun,
It's clear, the heart of nature sings.

Unfolding Layers of Existence

Digging through piles of twigs and leaves,
I found a worm that quipped, 'Hello!'
With shimmery eyes and a sassy smile,
He flaunted tales of the garden below.

I tried to count the ants in line,
But they laughed and scurried away.
"All for one!" they cheered in unison,
Leaving me in disarray.

A snail slid by, in a hurry, they said,
"Life's a race, or perhaps a crawl!"
I only blinked, wondering out loud,
How could they have such a ball?

Unfolding life, layer by layer,
I chuckle at every little find.
In this absurd dance of existence,
I wear the joy as my daily grind.

Portraits in the Open Air

A bee in a bowler hat,
Sipping from a daisy cup,
Winks at the introverted snail,
Who hides inside a cupcake.

A squirrel with a mustache,
Planning his next acorn heist,
Tips his tiny top hat,
To the jogger off to the east.

Clouds are just popcorn floating,
In a sky of blue jellybean,
While trees wear leafy berets,
Swaying to a breeze's tune.

The sun dons shades and sunscreen,
To avoid the moon's jealous glare,
As all the critters giggle,
Under the sky's vast purse.

The Seasons of Our Wandering

Spring pranks with blossoms bright,
Surprising us with pollen fights,
While summer swats at buzzing flies,
Wearing short shorts, oh what a sight!

Autumn's here with a snicker,
Leaves dive like a dance-off quick,
And winter, king of icy chills,
Hides snowballs in his frosty sleigh.

We skip from sun to snow so sweet,
While nature chuckles at our feet,
Oh, to wander like we're lost,
Discovering joy at any cost.

Seasons spin in a funny way,
Each moment's a vintage bouquet,
Who knew wormholes could be this grand?
With every turn, we make new plans.

Index of Nature's Secrets

Crickets compose, a symphony loud,
While frogs critique the tune with a croak,
Each leaf a page from the nature scroll,
Recording mischief, no one's bespoke.

Rabbits wear sophisticated ties,
And squirrels hold stock exchanges,
In the shade of the wise old oaks,
Where all the critters sound their ranges.

The moon's a giggling silver plate,
Serving dreams with a side of stars,
And fireflies write in glowing ink,
Charting paths that are really ours.

Nature holds jokes behind her veil,
In whispers soft, we laugh and wail,
As every rustle and chirp behaves,
Like a raucous party that never pales.

From Seed to Silence

From seedling sprout to leafy phase,
The garden hosts a multi-play,
Where carrots whisper underground,
And radishes stubbornly stay.

The sunflower stands, an eyebrow raised,
Judging how we dance and sway,
While peas form a conga line,
In a game they never play.

In stillness, secrets may unfold,
With worms reciting poetry bold,
As we ponder their wriggly ways,
And find the garden's tales retold.

From dirt to bloom, it's laughter's fault,
As nature crafts a world of salt,
In every silence, something stirs,
Between the lines where humor purls.

The Song of the Thistle

Beneath the sun, a thistle sways,
Waving at bees, in a clumsy ballet.
"Why don't you dance?" it teasingly jeers,
As ants trip over, shedding their fears.

A squirrel spins tales of nuts in his trove,
"I've got a secret, come on, let's rove!"
But the thistle just laughs, with a prickly grin,
"I'll keep the fun, while you search within."

Tickled by breezes, it hums a tune,
While shadows play games beneath the moon.
"Oh look! A hedgehog!" shouts the wayward sprout,
"I bet you can't guess what this fuss is about!"

In laughter and light, life crisscrosses fine,
Where the thistle keeps secrets, and wishes entwine.
With every misstep, and joy that it spills,
Nature's a jester, with unpredictable thrills.

Colors of An Unseen Horizon

Invisible shades lurk in the air,
Yellow and purple, so light, so rare.
A worm on a leaf sings an off-key song,
With a chorus of crickets chiming along.

The clouds wear pajamas of fluffy white fleece,
While daisies discuss quantum theories, at least.
Rabbits in bow ties conspire and plot,
What's up with that cow? It's just not that hot!

Sunsets hold whispers of pastel delight,
Each color a giggle, each hue a light fight.
The grasses hold secrets, some silly, some sly,
As I dance in the colors, I trip on the sky.

Behind every whisper, a chuckle awaits,
Each brushstroke of nature creates funny fates.
For hidden in laughter, and vibrant, full cheer,
The unseen horizon is actually here.

Notes in the Margins of Nature

A bunny writes poems in scribbles so bold,
Leaving little notes that never get old.
"Have you tried carrots?" one paper does share,
While another suggests naps under fresh air.

Ants hold a conference, debating their cheese,
No one can tell them they're tiny with ease.
A ladybug laughs, "You'll never believe,
This leaf is my kingdom, please don't misconceive!"

Raindrops have voices; they giggle and play,
Like whispers of kids who found chalk on the way.
The sun joins the fun, snickering bright,
While shadows compose symphonies, hidden from sight

With each little note, a chuckle embarks,
In the margins of nature, life scribbles its marks.
Each breeze brings a punchline, a twist of the fate,
In this wild, funny world, there's no need to wait.

The Shadowed Symphony

In the dusk, shadows stretch, forming a band,
An orchestra of misfits, at nature's command.
The trees sway and sway, like they're lost in a trance,
Chirping crickets lead, oh what a cha-cha dance!

A fox with a fiddle strums low with a grin,
While owls hoot the backup, in their soft, wise skin.
Each branch holds a joke, wrapped tight in a sigh,
As laughter echoes upward, into the night sky.

Beneath swirling leaves, where the fireflies twirl,
A melody blooms in a soft, silver swirl.
A raccoon in a tuxedo conducts with flair,
While the stars blink along, unaware and rare.

In the cool night air, as the shadows align,
Nature's sweet symphony carries a line.
With giggles and chirps, playful sounds so divine,
In the shadowed symphony, all things intertwine.

Ecology of the Unseen

In the grass I found a beetle,
Doing the cha-cha on my shoe.
A dance-off with a nearby ant,
They seemed to have quite the view.

A squirrel plucked my sandwich away,
With a smug grin, he made his escape.
I watched him, speechless in delight,
Eating like a tiny landscape scape.

The worms are wiggling with flair,
Debating on who's the best dressed.
With glistening coats of sludgy brown,
Not one of them won't jest at the rest.

And trees whisper secrets to the wind,
While grasshoppers play hide and seek.
Oh nature, in your hidden realms,
You make my worries feel quite weak.

Reverberations of Nature's Symphony

The frogs are crooning smooth serenades,
   While crickets manage the beat.
I joined in, a cacophony of quacks,
   My singing's quite the comical feat.

Bees buzz with their honeyed gossip,
   Plotting their next grand design.
I tiptoe close to catch their secrets,
   But end up tripping on a vine.

A robin hops in a top hat, how dapper!
   He struts like he owns the lawn.
I swear he winked at me with flair,
   His ego only slightly drawn.

Thunder rumbles with laughter above,
   Lightning dances, bright as a star.
In this wild jam session of the woods,
   Nature conducts, and I'm the bizarre.

The Unshackled Observer

I watched a rabbit with style so grand,
He wore tiny specs just to read.
With a book of carrots tucked in hand,
He giggled at me while I took heed.

A turtle zoomed past, or so I thought,
His chief headline was 'Speedy Slow'.
I cheered, 'You're the champion of this lot!'
But he smiled and seemed to steal the show.

Birds were sharing love notes up high,
In secret tweets, oh how they'd swoon.
I couldn't help but overhear,
What a gossiping bunch, the buffoons!

A raccoon joining in with a hat,
Declaring himself king of the night.
At that moment, I laughed so hard,
The critters had won the quirky fight.

Breath of the Untamed Earth

The clouds are tossing down confetti,
As raindrops tap dance on my head.
In puddles, frogs reign as royalty,
Splashing about like they're well-fed.

Mice in tuxedos scurry briskly,
To a soirée in the tall grass glade.
They waltz with fireflies like ballerinas,
What a whimsical masquerade!

Flowers compete in fashion shows,
With petals flowing, bright and bold.
A dandelion vows to be first,
In a crown of the day, proudly told.

The wind is giggling through the leaves,
With whispers that tickle my ears.
Nature's a playful, quirky jester,
Filling the world with joyful cheers.

Footprints of the Mind's Eye

In the garden of thought, I tripped,
Over ideas like scattered seeds,
Thoughts sprouting legs, running fast,
Chasing the sun, like it owes them money.

A squirrel stole my punchline,
Nibbled away while I pondered,
Did it laugh or just chatter away?
Mental acrobatics, without a mat.

Clouds giggle, whispering secrets,
While ants stage a tiny play,
I'm just the audience, bemused,
Taking notes on their hilarious ways.

Caught in a daze of silly sights,
Chasing shadows that dance on grass,
Each misstep a good punchline,
Who knew my thoughts could be this clumsy?

The Network of Roots

Beneath the surface, the chatter grows,
Roots gossip like old friends at a café,
"Who's got the juiciest fruit this season?"
They trade secrets, like tradesmen on break.

Worms throw a wild dance party,
Inviting beetles with shiny shoes,
A ruckus beneath the rustling leaves,
Life's a game, who knew so many played?

Mud puddles are their dance floors,
Every splash a riotous cheer,
While daisies roll their eyes above,
"Oh, grow up, dear roots, it's time to chill!"

Branches laugh, isolating up high,
Echoing love songs of the ground,
Where down below, the mischief thrives,
Roots, a tangled web of wisecracks.

A Tapestry Woven by the Wind

The wind spins tales like a storyteller,
Sewing laughter into every gust,
A kite's journey is a comedy,
Loop-de-loops and snags, oh what fun!

Leaves rustle, clapping their applause,
As clouds take turns at punchlines,
"Did you see that tree's dance?" they joke,
A ballet of branches—who knew they twirled?

Feathers float down like soft confetti,
Whispers of birds caught in the act,
They chirp out riddles in the breeze,
Nesting curiosity, a crowd pleaser.

Every gust a new narrative spun,
Through the open fields, stories roam,
Laughter stitched within every tale,
The wind, a jester, never alone.

Echoes in the Meadow

In the meadow, echoes bounce back,
A sheep bleats "Baa!" and goats reply,
Each sound a joke thrown into the air,
Even crickets chuckle in cadence.

Butterflies flaunt their vibrant puns,
Landing on flowers like gossip spread,
"Did you hear what the rogue bee said?"
Nature's theater, where mirth abounds.

Sunlight flickers, a playful wink,
Illuminating the laughter of grass,
As ants march to their own beat,
A tiny parade of humor on the move.

Every echo a giggle reframed,
Resounding through the soft stillness,
Meadow life, a comedic ensemble,
Where even silence can't help but chuckle.

Untamed Connections

In the brush, a squirrel sneezes,
Dropping acorns like rain.
A raccoon gives the side-eye,
"Watch where you step, that's my lane!"

The deer prance, they're quite the dancers,
Two left hooves on swampy ground.
A grasshopper takes his chances,
With moves that know no bound!

Birds chirp gossip, quite amusing,
About the chipmunk's latest snack.
And in the mix, the bees are cruising,
Sweet chaos is the way back!

Nature's circus, no time for fuss,
Each critter playing their part.
With giggles, we join in the bus,
In the wild, we're all heart.

The Quiet Currents of Life

In the river, fish throw a party,
Bubbles rise, they dance on air.
A otter slides down, quite hearty,
Laughing as he gulps a pear!

The frogs are croaking out their tune,
A chorus straight from the swamp.
They'll serenade beneath the moon,
While the dragonflies just romp!

Turtles play slow-poke, that's their style,
As crickets keep the score.
They hop and twang with greatest guile,
While laughter echoes from the shore.

And as dusk settles, stars ignite,
Nature's jesters keep the show.
In every ripple, life feels right,
As chuckles in the twilight flow.

Reflections on Rough Terrain

Stumbling over roots and stones,
Laughter spills like fresh spring rain.
A skunk nearby is striking poses,
"Just smell my flowers, what a gain!"

A tumbleweed rolls by in glee,
While I trip over a thorn.
The sudden jolt, oh dear me!
Got a new dance move, I'm reborn!

The rocks start chatting, oh so wise,
"You should really watch where you go!"
But I just grin and roll my eyes,
"Thanks rocks, but I steal the show!"

Each footstep slips, yet fun won't cease,
With giggles echoing today.
Rough terrain can still bring peace,
And joy leads me all the way.

Symbiosis in the Wild Air

Up in trees, the squirrels jest,
Trading tricks with crafty crows.
A game of hide-and-seek, no rest,
In nature's wild, the fun just grows!

Bees are buzzing, sharing thrills,
"Hey, look! I've found the sweetest spot!"
While ants march on, they have the skills,
Making sure no crumbs are caught.

Butterflies flit in a grand ballet,
Colors clash in joyful flight.
An awkward hop from a snail's sway,
Adds to the dance, pure delight!

Together we'll weave this sunny thread,
Life stitched tight with laughter's power.
In the wild air, worries shed,
Let's celebrate nature's hour.

A Dance Among the Shadows

In the garden's heart, we twirl,
Chasing shadows, making whirl.
The daisies giggle as we pass,
While crickets cheer in green grass.

With a wink, the sun spins round,
Grasshoppers leap, all joy is found.
We juggle weeds like silly clowns,
Wearing dirt masks, no golden crowns.

Frogs croak jokes in nearby pools,
While we strut like bumbling fools.
A butterfly flaps with a sly grin,
And we clap our hands, let's begin!

As twilight whispers through the trees,
Our dance continues with the breeze.
The stars join in, a twinkling crowd,
In this shadowed ball, we're always loud.

Echoes Beneath the Canopy

Beneath the leaves, a secret's told,
Where whispers of the ancient unfold.
Squirrels gossip in acorn attire,
While chipmunks exchange their wildest fire.

Bouncing twigs, a tangle of fun,
Nature's hide-and-seek has begun.
A raccoon squints, with a crafty face,
As we stumble yearn to keep pace.

Our laughter echoes, bouncing about,
While mushrooms giggle, without a doubt.
We strike a pose, oh what a sight,
As shadows dance into the night.

The canopy sways, a leafy cheer,
Our voices rising, loud and clear.
Here among the branches we perform,
In Mother Earth's chaotic, warm storm.

Where Soil Meets Sky

Digging deep, we find lost toys,
Forgotten trinkets from girls and boys.
With each scoop, the past comes alive,
In dirt, we flourish, and we thrive.

With a shovel, we plan our quests,
Against the roots, nature's tests.
A worm wiggles, giving grand advice,
'In the world of soil, it's quite nice!'

We plant a dream straight into the ground,
Expecting magic to spin around.
Sunlight laughs at our wild guess,
While clouds wander, seeking success.

As we wait for the sprout to rise,
The ants giggle beneath our sighs.
Oh, to watch the miracle unfold,
In a garden where stories are told.

Flux and Flow of Earthly Rhythms

Rhythms beat in the chest of the earth,
As we gather in laughter, give rebirth.
The wind whispers secrets in our ears,
While tiny beetles dance without fears.

Jumping puddles, splashes galore,
With our boots, we rumble and roar.
Raindrops chime a merry tune,
Underneath the watchful moon.

Roots wiggle in rhythm with glee,
As flowers sway with raucous esprit.
It's a party where soil shakes hands,
And nature smiles across the lands.

With each step, we rock and sway,
To the green beats that lead the way.
Under stars, our spirits intertwine,
Joy flows free, in this wild design.

Conversations with the Wilderness

Whispers in the trees, a squirrel's witty quip,
A raccoon remarks, with a smirk on its lip.
The brook chuckles softly, a gurgling laugh,
As I try to explain why I've lost my path.

The chipmunk rolls its eyes at my GPS plight,
While the owl hoots loudly, 'You'll be here all night!'
I step on a twig, and the forest erupts,
A cacophony of giggles as nature erupts.

My hat's on a bush, the wind gives a cheer,
The flowers laugh loudly, "We've been waiting here!"
With wildlife as jesters, I dance on the ground,
In this quirky circus, absurdity's found.

The Pulse of Quiet Moments

Amid the stillness, a breeze starts to tease,
As butterflies jig – look, they're dancing with ease!
A snail is my coach, 'Go slow, don't you rush,'
While ants stage a race – it's a tiny big hush.

In the pond, frogs croak out an opera so grand,
While the sun grins down, a spotlight on land.
I attempt to meditate, but a grasshopper leaps,
With all of its flair, my calmness it keeps.

Mushrooms are whispering secrets so sly,
And I join in the chatter, just me and the sky.
The wind's got jokes, it rustles my hair,
As I giggle with daisies, all carefree and rare.

Stitches in the Tapestry of Time

Each leaf tells a story, stitched bright and bold,
In a quilt made of sunshine, and laughter retold.
The clouds are my mentors in this playful craft,
As they unravel their shapes, the laughter is daft.

Pinecones drop down like little surprise gifts,
While ladybugs chuckle, "Hey, check out our lifts!"
A breeze pulls my scarf, 'You can't quite sew me,'
As I chase after threads of this wild jubilee.

Time's a mischievous seamstress, with stitches awry,
But I grin at the chaos, let out a loud sigh.
For every misstep is a moment of cheer,
In this patchwork of life, I hold dear what I hear.

Chronicles of an Open Sky

Clouds swap stories like gossiping friends,
As they morph into shapes, where the laughing never ends.
A plane zooms above, drawing laughter so bright,
While I wave at the birds, who are taking flight.

The moon peeks out, with a wink and a smile,
And stars join the fun, let's play for a while!
The sun spills its colors, like paints that run free,
While horizons giggle with gleeful esprit.

try to catch rainbows, but they slip through my hands,
As the sky whispers secrets of whimsical lands.
Laughter of nature, in the great open air,
In the chronicles woven, joy is laid bare.

Reverberations of the Untamed

In the meadow, cows wear shades,
As they gossip about their hay days.
A goat on a roof, acting like a king,
While birds chuckle, sharing gossip in the spring.

Jumping jacks with the ants, can you believe?
They dance to a tune, we all want to leave.
A fruit bat swoops, oh what a sight,
Stealing snacks from picnics, taking flight!

The creek giggles as it flows along,
Making up verses, joining the song.
Frogs complete the chorus, so out of tune,
While turtles sunbathe, basking till noon.

Laughter echoes through grass and trees,
Nature's carnival, a joyful breeze.
Forget the rules, let wonders align,
In this wild spectacle, everything's fine.

Traces of a Thundering Heartbeat

Thunderous drums from a distant cloud,
A squirrel reenacts a parade, so proud.
Lightning bugs blink like they're on the stage,
And the rain, oh the rain, brings an end to the page.

Clouds in shapes of elephants and cheese,
While rabbits hold sneaky meetings in threes.
They plot secret missions, perhaps a heist,
To steal the last cookie at a summer feast.

The wind whispers secrets behind trees so grand,
As a cat sings karaoke, holding the band.
The branches sway as they carry the tune,
And even the moon is tapping—who knew?

Giggles of raindrops splash on the floor,
Nature's own comedy, we can't ignore.
With each heartbeat, laughter takes flight,
In this chaotic symphony, day turns to night.

Harvesting Echos

A scarecrow twirls, what a funky sight,
Pretending to dance in the soft moonlight.
Crows join the party, dressed in their best,
As veggies roll in on a train to invest.

Pumpkins gossip about their big dreams,
While beetles debate the weight of their creams.
The cornfield sways, chuckling aloud,
As farmers take bets, trying hard not to shout.

Fluffy clouds drift like cotton candy soft,
While goats scamper up, shaking off the loft.
A tractor plays tunes, country's in line,
As tractors and toads share a wild wine.

The harvest of humor fuels every laugh,
In this rural playground, nature's a craft.
So bring your sunshine, and dance till the end,
With echoes of joy, on every bend!

The Wanderer's Canvas

With crayons made of earth, a palette of glee,
A wanderer sprinkles colors from trees.
Splashing mud puddles, a daring ballet,
Even the rain wants to join in the play.

A fox in a scarf takes a stroll on the lane,
While flowers wear hats, laughing without shame.
The rocks tell stories of adventures gone by,
As clouds form critiques, floating up high.

The world's a canvas where laughter is caught,
As giggling rivers weave tales on the spot.
A sunbeam giggles, dances on grass,
While shadows draw cartoons of moments that pass.

So let's wander free, with whimsy as our guide,
Life is a masterpiece, not just a ride.
With each crooked line, let joy be our stance,
In this gallery of life, come join the dance!

A Poem in the Breeze

The wind sings songs of yore,
While I chase my hat on the floor.
A squirrel snickers up a tree,
As if he's mocking me for free.

Fluffy clouds roll by like sheep,
I trip on roots; oh, what a leap!
Nature laughs, it's a grand show,
With grass stains on my pants to show.

Sifting Through Nature's Scrapbook

I found a leaf that turned to brown,
It whispered secrets; made me frown.
A bug named Fred held up a sign,
Said, 'Don't be shy, come join the line!'

Old twigs pose like sticks of art,
Laughing at my clumsy heart.
A dandelion, with cheeky flair,
Challenged me to dance and dare.

The Interstice of Color and Shade

Bees do the tango by the rose,
While ants parade in tiny clothes.
A rainbow spills across the grass,
As children giggle and try to pass.

Puddles reflect the sky so blue,
I tiptoe 'round, like clumsy goo.
A dragonfly dives with a wink,
I blink back at him—oh, what a link!

An Invitation to Observe

Grab your boots and join the parade,
Where worms do yoga in the glade.
A multitude of critters shout,
'You've missed a fun day, come without a doubt!'

I question dandelions, 'Is it true?
Are you the stars that fell right through?'
Laughter bubbles up from a brook,
A perfect spot with nature's book.

Patches of Earthbound Votes

A worm wears glasses, looking quite wise,
Debating with ants about who sells fries.
The sun shines bright on their tiny backs,
As they plot their escapades over lunch snacks.

A grasshopper jumps, claiming his fame,
Saying, 'I could hop further, what's your name?'
The ladybug laughs, her spots all aglow,
'Let's settle this dance, in a row!'

Bees buzz with gossip, secrets unfold,
Tales of flower theft and treasures of gold.
As they shape a buzzworthy voting con,
In a world where petals sway until dawn.

The daisies nod as bards sing their tune,
In the meadow, they party til late afternoon.
With patches of earth where mischief ignites,
Their hilarity echoes on warm summer nights.

Secrets Among the Ferns

In the shade of the ferns, where whispers converge,
A snail tells a tale, her feelings surge.
She dreams of a race against the swift wind,
But jokes on her shell, life's fun at the end.

Mice play poker, using acorns for chips,
With cards made of leaves, they exchange little quips.
A hedgehog bets all, with a snicker and grin,
While fireflies flash to signal their win.

The old wise owl hoots, 'What's this discourse?'
As they plot and they scheme, taking turns with no remorse.
Joking and laughing through the night sky,
These secrets of ferns could make anyone cry.

As dawn breaks the laughter drifts soft with the breeze,
While shadows retreat, the birds sing with ease.
Those daytime secrets will soon be forgot,
In a forest of laughter, the ferns' funny plot.

The Mutable Horizon

Clouds were julienned, sliced up with a knife,
While the sun sipped coffee and pondered on life.
In a world where horizons could bend and twist,
The sky proclaimed, 'Let's make a big list!'

The moon wore a hat, with stars all agleam,
Saying, 'I'm more than night; I'm the daytime's dream!
A comet freeloaded, caught rides on the breeze,
Navigating through galaxies like conquering tease.

Rivers jumped over the stones, wearing shades,
Singing complaints about silly charades.
In the land where the earth tickles the stars,
The mutable horizon is where humor goes far.

Fill your cup with laughter, as odd shapes collide,
In a whimsical world where jokes never hide.
With boundless horizons, each chuckle's a thrill,
Arranging tomorrow; it's a comedy drill.

Visions on the Backroads of Thought

Nonsense signposts guide us through brain's maze,
Where the thoughts drift like mist on a funny phase.
A detour for giggles, a shortcut for glee,
As wisdom takes naps beneath the old tree.

Two geese in sunglasses start a debate,
About which way's best to attract a good fate.
While squirrels take bets on who'll yell the loudest,
And the trees lean in, feeling quite proudest.

A road paved with laughter leads nowhere on maps,
Yet squirrels with backpacks organize their mishaps.
With each twist and turn, the odd gets doubled,
In the backroads of thought, no one stays troubled.

Chasing after whimsies, embracing the sway,
Visions emerge that brighten the day.
Amongst all this wonder, joy takes a seat,
And life writes its script, oh so bittersweet!

Driftwood of Thoughts

Wandering thoughts like driftwood,
Sometimes lost in a stream of dreams.
Chasing squirrels and their nutty plans,
I wonder if they have little schemes.

A frog jumps up to greet the sun,
With a bow, he steals the spotlight right.
The breeze joins in, a playful dance,
While I giggle at this silly sight.

A rabbit dashes like a comet,
With a mission, no time to spare.
Do they know I'm laughing loudly?
Or is the joke too much to bear?

So I sit, as clouds drift by,
A comical cast in nature's play.
Life's oddities make me chuckle,
In this wild theatre, I'll stay.

The Texture of Wildness

Rolling hills like lumpy dough,
Covered in patches of cheeky green.
A goat looks back, with a knowing wink,
As if it's the king of this scene.

The trees wear hats of mossy hair,
And giggle when the wind blows cold.
Squirrels throw acorns like confetti,
Parties in the woods, oh so bold!

I trip over roots with a flair,
The ground laughs softly, how rude!
But a porcupine snickers with pride,
In this wild place, nothing's subdued.

The rocks stand guard, stoic and still,
With secrets that they refuse to share.
But I'll keep poking and prodding,
For humor hides in every square.

Observations from the Mist

Mist hangs low like an awkward guest,
Sneaking in, where it shouldn't be.
It swirls around, a playful tease,
Catching the trees in a mystery.

A deer peeks out like it's on stage,
With a spotlight, it strikes a pose.
Did it know I was watching close?
Or is it part of a grand show?

The grass giggles underfoot,
Tickling my toes with every step.
And I laugh as puddles mimic me,
In a game that I never prepped.

So I frolic with the foggy crew,
Each shadow a friend in this charade.
Together we dance, laugh, and play,
In the misty world, the best parade.

Imprints on the Soft Ground

Footprints trailing like a ribbon,
Marking the paths of wanderlust.
Each print tells tales of clumsy joys,
In a dance we did that we must trust.

A raccoon joins, with paws in the mix,
Digging here and scratching there.
Whiskers twitch in the soft mud,
A jolly bandit, beyond compare.

I see the imprints of a bee,
Dancing wildly between petals bright.
Did it sip just to loosen up?
Or is it buzzing from pure delight?

So I tread softly, making my mark,
In this canvas of laughter and fun.
Every step a giggle waiting to burst,
In a world where silly has just begun.

Gazing into the Eyes of the Unknown

With a map that makes no sense,
I wander through the tall grass.
A deer stares back, quite bemused,
Is it lost too, or just playing smart?

Butterflies take bets on my next step,
As I trip over my own two feet.
A crow caws loudly, what a critic!
I give it a wave, then lose my treat.

A squirrel dashes by, all fluff and charm,
Accusing me of intruding here.
Its gaze is sharp, a tiny alarm,
I laugh it off, feeling no fear.

At last, I spot a tree that's bent,
Whispering secrets to the wind.
I ask for wisdom, it merely scents,
And tells me my hair still needs a trim!

Footprints on the Forgotten Path

There's a path where the brambles dance,
And crickets sing in cheeky tones.
I tread lightly, imagine it a chance,
But stumble right into the gnomes' homes.

They peek out from their leafy lairs,
With hats quite odd and weathered tongues.
I swear I heard them share some glares,
And then they broke into silly songs.

A frog joins in, quite out of tune,
Swapping my jokes for a ribbit or two.
Together we croak 'neath the lazy moon,
Making memories, a delightful brew.

As I leave, I hear a distant cheer,
The gnomes and frogs now best of pals.
Next time I'm here, I'll bring some beer,
To celebrate with them, oh what jolly gals!

The Dance of Flora and Fauna

In a meadow where daisies twirl,
I spot the bees throw a buzzing ball.
They're lively, hopping in floral swirl,
While a nearby snail takes its slow crawl.

A tortoise breaks into a grand jig,
Laughing at critters that rush all around.
It winks at a frog who leaps like a pig,
I must admit, the dance is profound!

The trees, they sway, cheerleaders in green,
Each leaf applauding the odd display.
Clouds float above, enjoying the scene,
"Nature's got talent," they sweetly say.

As I join in, the sun starts to sink,
The meadow erupts in a burst of light.
I wonder what thoughts the flowers think,
As day turns to dusk, and I giggle with delight!

Harvesting Shadows and Light

I wandered deep where shadows blend,
With sunlight sneaking through the trees.
Caught a glimpse of a ghostly friend,
Who winked and danced with the evening breeze.

The oak roots twisted like a riddle,
I tried to untangle their whispering words.
But the light played tricks, oh what a fiddle,
Leading me to a cluster of birds.

They squawked a tune about snacks and seeds,
While I fumbled for bites in my pack.
Realized then, maybe they had needs,
A feast fit for a snacker's attack.

So we shared crumbs as the shadows flared,
Laughter fell like dew on the ground.
In the dance of dusk, nothing was spared,
We were all silly, lighthearted, and unbound!

Whispers of the Untamed

In the thicket, squirrels debate,
Nuts or acorns, which one's first rate?
The deer giggle with flawless grace,
As raccoons raid every picnic place.

The birds gossip in bright feathered chat,
"Is that a human? I'm sure of that!"
While frogs take bets in a noisy croak,
Contemplating if today's the day to joke.

A lone fox prances past the trees,
Singing showtunes with relative ease.
Beneath the sun, nature knows her lines,
A grand performance, where laughter twines.

So come along, join this buoyant spree,
Where every leaf has a story, you see.
In this wild room where antics abound,
The laughs are plenty, and joy is found.

Notes from the Edge of Observation

With binoculars, I spy on a thrush,
Whose awkward dance begins with a hush.
The butterfly flops like it's had too much,
While ants form a line; oh, what a clutch!

A raccoon in shades makes quite the scene,
Moonlighting, it's sure, in a heist routine.
While bees wear hats, or so it appears,
Buzzing about with sweet covert cheers.

On a branch, an owl with a bemused eye,
Judges the show as it drifts on by.
"Please, no selfies!" it hoots with great flair,
While the sun sets in a gold-hued glare.

Watch me take notes as I laugh and stare,
At this quirky cast unaware I'm there.
Nature's sitcom, lined up just right,
In the theater of day, under glittering night.

Nature's Quiet Chronicles

Grass blades whisper of gossip benign,
While mushrooms plot at the edge of the pine.
A snail races; what's he in a rush for?
Behind him, a worm shouts, "Hey, I'm the tour!"

The stream chuckles, tickling stones in glee,
As tadpoles navigate their own little spree.
Bubbles of laughter dance up to the sky,
While clouds look down, wondering why.

Butterflies swish in a color parade,
In a toss-up of who's the brightest displayed.
Each snapshot taken, a joyful delight,
As the moods shift from daytime to night.

So take off your shoes, step into this play,
Where nature's chapters unfold every day.
Bring a pinch of laughter and sprinkle it wide,
Through the quirky tales where wild fun resides.

The Heartbeat of Wild Places

In meadows where daisies twirl in delight,
A bunny hops with vertical might.
He pauses to check the grass for a snack,
With a wiggly nose that's got no lack.

A hedgehog rolls like it's in a spree,
Bumping into a very confused bee.
Fluffy clouds join in a puffy parade,
While the sun throws confetti with every grade.

Lizards bask, strutting their stunning shine,
Posing like pros, with shoulders divine.
The wind carries giggles, both crisp and bright,
As frogs do their croaking, highlighting the night.

Join the frenzy, live it untamed,
Where nature's rhythm has never been tamed.
With each heartbeat of wild, our spirits align,
In this zoo of hilarity, the world feels just fine.

Wandering Through Uncharted Lands

I stroll through grass, knee-high and green,
My compass spins like a wild machine.
Who knew a twig could cause such a fall?
Nature laughs, saying, 'That's not your call!'

Bugs play tag on my shiny new hat,
A squirrel gives me the side-eye, how 'bout that?
I wave to the flowers, they wave back too,
Oh look, a rock! Is it a pet? Who knew!

Voices of the Earth Beneath My Feet

Each step I take, the ground does speak,
Whispers of worms with secrets to leak.
A mole pokes his head: 'What's all this fuss?'
I shrug, 'Just curious, don't make a fuss!'

Gravel crunches like popcorn under my toes,
The daisies giggle, in secret, it shows.
I bow down low to hear their sweet song,
But trip on a root—oh where did I go wrong?

The Rhythm of Untamed Soil

The soil dances, a waltz full of cheer,
With every step, the earth sings loud and clear.
A pair of old boots join the lively beat,
Tap dancing with ants, oh what a feat!

Worms twist and twirl, forming a chain,
'Come join us!' they call, and I don't refrain.
But wait—what's that? A shoe stuck in mud?
Looks like I'm now part of this dancing thud!

Whispers from the Wind

The breeze carries tales of socks on a line,
It tickles my ear, says, 'Try lemon-lime!'
I shout to the clouds, 'Hold on for a sec!'
But they just roll on, what the heck?

Laughing leaves agree; it's a party up there,
With everyone mingling, no need for a care.
I twirl with the daisies, like a silly old fool,
Nature's the teacher, and I'm the kid in school!

Wandering Through the Unwritten

I tripped on a thought, oh what a surprise,
A dance with the grass, under wide-open skies.
The writing is messy, my notes all askew,
As I pondered life's questions, wearing one shoe.

Nibbles from squirrels, they steal all my snacks,
While I wear a hat that I think looks like wax.
Chasing my shadows, they flee with a grin,
Maybe today I just won't let them win.

The trees whisper secrets, they giggle and sway,
My journal's a riot, with doodles at play.
I sketched out a monster, gave it a top hat,
And suddenly it's leading a parade with a cat.

But alas, the sun sets, the laughter it wanes,
As I gather my treasures, some twigs and some grains.
I wander on home, with a smile and a fumble,
In this unwritten world, where I bumble and tumble.

Voices of the Ancient Grove

The trees conspire, whispering glee,
Inviting me deeper, come play, you'll see!
A squirrel in a toga, he's leading the charge,
With branches for trumpets, they play music large.

Echoes of laughter, from roots underground,
Where mushrooms are dancing, all jumbled around.
A wise old oak, wearing spectacles quaint,
Recounts all the tales that no human could paint.

I spotted a shadow, a flicker of feet,
Turns out it's a raccoon, selling candy to eat.
The ghosts of the forest, they peek through the trees,
Sharing grape juice and nuts, with a dash of pure breeze.

Oh, the prancing and leaping, a sight to behold,
This grove of delights, where the ancient are bold.
With laughter like ripples, and joy at the core,
In this happy old grove, I just can't help but explore!

Cartography of the Unfamiliar

Maps that are wobbly, drawn with spaghetti,
I thought I'd explore, but now I'm quite sweaty.
With a compass that spins like a cat on a spree,
Where's north? Is it under the big old oak tree?

Sandwiches scattered, all over the map,
I'll never find dinner; I'm caught in this trap!
With each step I take, there's giggles abound,
The terrain shifts to jello, I'm stuck on the ground.

A patchwork of colors, a cuppa in hand,
Nestled under clouds that look like a band.
I charted a course, through fields ripe with sass,
Where the flowers all gossip, and the daisies all pass.

Adventure's absurd, but I walk with a grin,
Finding joy in the chaos, where laughter begins.
These silly adventures, no need for a guide,
In the cartography of worlds where I abide!

In the Fold of Silence

Whispers of quiet, as soft as a sigh,
Sipping at shadows beneath a blue sky.
A ladybug giggles, as she rides on a breeze,
While I ponder the meaning of ants and their cheese.

The stillness is thick, but I like it just fine,
As I stilt-walk in circles, pretending to dine.
The flowers are peeking, their petals all pried,
As I wave at the cactus who secretly cried.

I caught a reflection in a puddle so small,
It winked back at me, and said, "You've got gall!"
The wind tossed my notes like confetti in flight,
And I laughed at the chaos that burst into night.

In a quiet that tickles like bubbles in air,
I found all the joy in the moments laid bare.
For in silence there's humor, a giggle, a pause,
Where I weave all my tales, with no need for applause.

The Unfurling Grass

The grass stands up with glee,
Tickling the toes of passersby.
Each step a wobbly dance,
Nature's pranks, oh how they vie!

Dandelions blowing bubbles,
Whispers of laughter in the breeze.
Bugs slide down blades like slides,
A ballet for ants, if you please!

Knees hit the ground, muddy and happy,
The earth sighs in joyous embrace.
With each hill a rollercoaster,
Smiles bloom on every face!

Chasing shadows, we play tag,
Time stands still in this green maze.
With every laugh, we grow younger,
The grass knows all our silly ways.

An Anthology of Footsteps

A parade of feet on this dusty trail,
Each step a story waiting to unveil.
From stompers to tiptoes, all join in line,
A conga of soles, divine!

There's a squelch from the puddles, a slap and a squish,
With a risk of muddy shoes, but who cares? We wish!
A toddler with glee leaps, welcoming the rain,
While some dodge droplets like they're playing a game!

The squirrels point and chuckle at everyone here,
As shoes stick to shoes, in the dance of the near.
A flip and a flop, we slip in a bind,
All in good fun, it's the joy we find!

We scribble our paths on this blank terrain,
Footprints like ink on a green-stained page.
With laughter forming the words in our wake,
An anthology of fun, let's revel and shake!

Footsteps on the Canvas of Earth

With each toe, a brushstroke, a quirky design,
We paint the path where the wildflowers shine.
Strawberries hide in the tall grass they call,
As we stomp through the field, we're bound to fall!

Each footprint a masterpiece, carefree and bold,
Little artists roam, let the laughter unfold.
A tug from a shrub, 'Hey, don't you dare leave!'
The plants have fun tricks, oh, woeful reprieve!

In this splattered-green art, giggles collide,
Making mud pies with unbridled pride.
Laughter erupts as a breeze shuffles through,
Tickling our noses with floral debut!

So let's scrapbook our footprints, the moments they hold,
With stories like vines, we'll weave through the gold.
Each step we take marks a joyful affair,
On this canvas of earth, we frolic and share!

The Journey Through Tangled Paths

In a maze of mischief, we walk side by side,
Twisting our way with characters wild.
Under tree branches that gently conspire,
Whispering secrets—oh, how they conspire!

My friend claims the bushes are out to get us,
As a branch gently swipes—oh, what a fuss!
Navigating hedges that giggle and sway,
Like a game of tag on an unpredictable day.

With every step forward, hilarity grows,
Laughter erupts as the underbrush knows.
The squirrels look down with high-pitched shrieks,
Counting our blunders and wobbly sneaks!

So onward, we trudge with a comical flair,
Through tangled paths and the fresh country air.
The journey is silly, with memories to seek,
In the woods where we laugh, let's take it out peak!

Transitory Moments in Nature

A squirrel jumped, then slipped,
On a branch that wasn't there.
Nature's comedy troupe performs,
With giggles hidden in the air.

Butterflies dance, oh so clumsy,
Like toddlers on a sugar high.
Chasing flowers, then prone to trip,
As bees buzz by with a sly sigh.

An ant in uniform, marching proud,
Lost its path—it's a comic show!
He's the general of the lost,
In the land of nearly so.

The wind whispers jokes to the grass,
While clouds play hide and seek above.
Nature rolls its eyes with glee,
It's all a hilarious dance of love.

Textures Beneath Bare Feet

Oh, the joy of grass and mud,
A tickle underfoot, so sly.
One moment smooth, the next a puddle,
Splashing with a laugh and a sigh.

Pebbles underfoot, a little sting,
Like nature's way of saying, 'Hey!'
Each step a treasure for the soles,
In this chaotic ballet.

Sticky sap and crunchy leaves,
What a dance upon the ground!
Every step a riddle wrapped,
In giggles and whispers profound.

Let's not forget the prickly thorns,
Oh, what a fun surprise!
A leap of faith leaves us howling,
As laughter meets our startled cries.

The Architecture of Silence

Whispers become a playful tease,
In a world that holds its breath.
The trees conspire with the breeze,
Plotting a joke of quiet death.

A rock sits solemn, like a wise sage,
While beetles write their memoirs near.
But suddenly, a sneeze unpaged,
And nature bursts with laughter and cheer.

Mushrooms huddle, gossiping low,
Sharing secrets, soft and sweet.
In silence, they laugh like pros,
As a snail slides by, shuffling its feet.

Even the sun, in fleeting rays,
Seems to chuckle at the scene.
Creating shadows, weaving plays,
In the architecture of the unseen.

Luminescence of Forgotten Corners

A lamp post flickers like a wink,
In corners where shadows misbehave.
It sighs and giggles, you would think,
That mischief's hiding in its cave.

Old bricks smile, chipped and grand,
Observing life's circus from their height.
They chat of days that were unplanned,
Under the cover of the night.

Rusty pipes dance, clattering tunes,
As rats tap their tiny feet.
Echoes of laughter beneath the moon,
The urban wildlife's late night beat.

In these corners, laughter glows,
With stories floating in the air.
Each flicker, crackle—life bestows,
The funny business everywhere.

Navigating the Currents of Life

Paddling through puddles, splashes fly,
Ducks quack like they own the sky.
With maps made of crumpled fast-food bags,
We dodge the mud like a couple of rags.

Frogs leap like they've found a spring sale,
With their croaks, they craft an odd tale.
Which way is up? I forgot to check,
But my GPS says, 'Turn, what the heck!'

I trip over roots that laugh in glee,
They know my clumsiness all too well, see?
Navigating chaos, both big and small,
Life's a river; we're just riding the sprawl.

As we whirl in circles, join the parade,
Smiling and laughing at every charade.
For in these currents, both wild and bright,
We find the humor in the muddled plight.

Roots that Breathe and Bloom

Roots underground whisper sweet lies,
Claiming they know what springs up to rise.
With a tickle and tease, they start to sway,
Making the grass dance in the sun's bright play.

Each flower's a joke that nature made,
Blooming in colors like it's a charade.
Bees buzzing around like they're auditioning,
For the role of the buzz that's most fitting.

Gathering pollen, the insects take turns,
In this wild comedy, our laughter burns.
Plants stretching arms like they're ready to hug,
But watch out, I think that one's a bug!

Even the weeds think they're a big deal,
Claiming the garden is theirs to steal.
In this riot of growth, with roots that loom,
We all find our place to breathe and bloom.

Lighthouses of Distant Landscape

Beacons blinking as I trip the light,
Chasing shadows that dance in the night.
With a sandwich shield, I march through the mist,
Daring the seagulls to bring up their twist.

Towering high, those lighthouses grin,
Watching me stumble, wishing to win.
"Turn left at the wave, take a step to the right,"
I'd rather follow the stars; they'll guide my flight.

Drifting and laughing, the waves are my cheer,
As seagulls squawk, "Why are you here?"
Navigating giggles on rocky terrain,
The salty air tickles, it's hard to complain.

With each crashing wave, I find my way,
In this lighthouse laughter, I'll choose to stay.
For in the distance, life shines bold and true,
As I navigate this wacky ocean view.

Listening to the Heart of the Soil

The ground grumbles softly, what's on its mind?
As worms wiggle by, they're one of a kind.
Each burrow they make, a secretive plot,
Tickling the roots like they're all that we've got.

Composting dreams in the pit of the earth,
Where sprouting ideas take root from their birth.
I lean down to listen, it sighs with delight,
Turning the mundane into paths of light.

Here's a potato with tales to tell,
Of sprightly adventures beneath the shell.
While carrots gossip, they wiggle and pry,
"Root for us!" they shout, "Do you see us fly?"

With each little heartbeat beneath sturdy feet,
The soil whispers jokes that can't be beat.
So I laugh with the plants as they flourish and toil,
In this warm embrace, I hear the heart of the soil.

www.ingramcontent.com/pod-product-compliance
Lightning Source LLC
Chambersburg PA
CBHW051642160426
43209CB00004B/760